# REPTILES

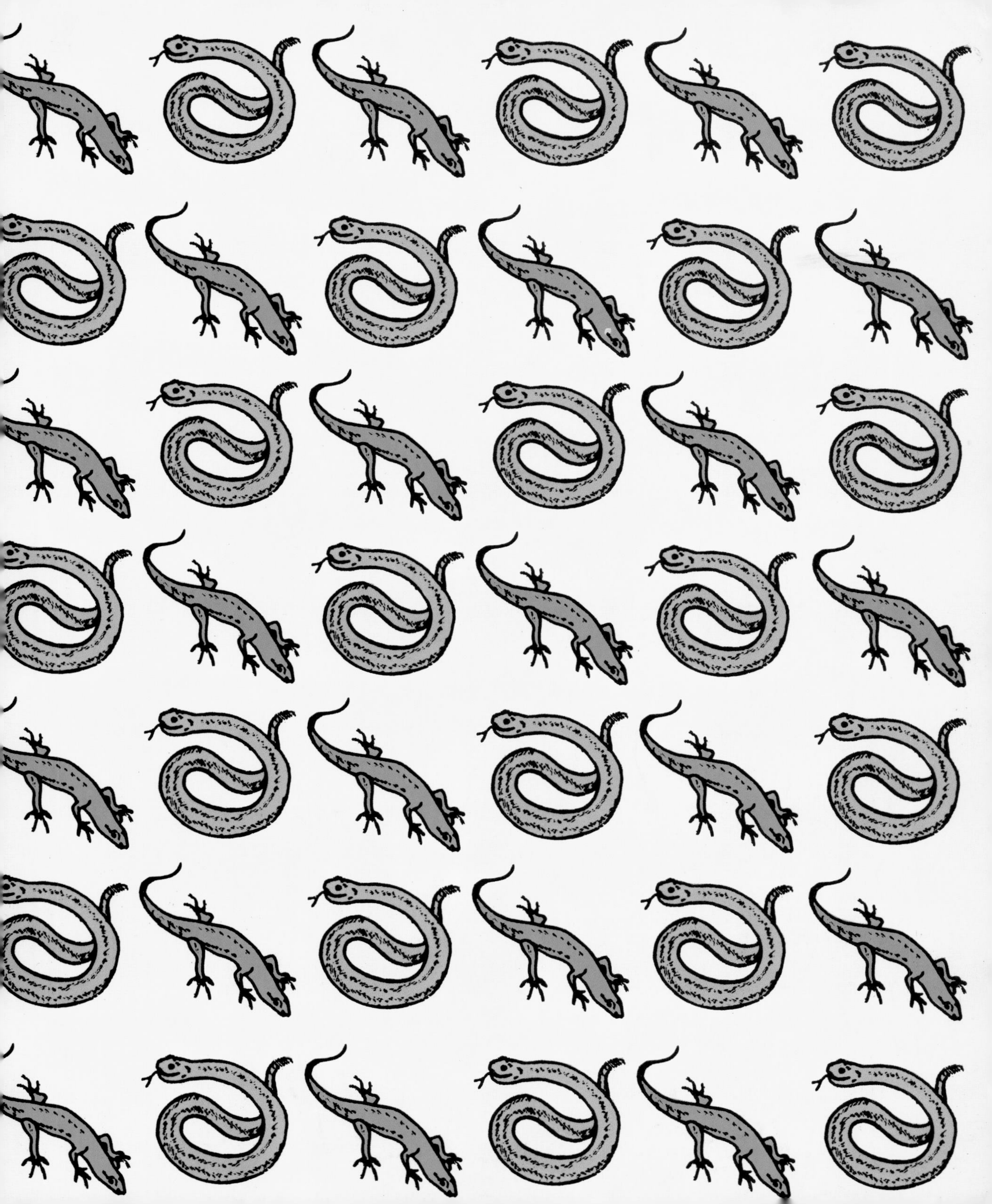

Franklin Watts, Inc.
95 Madison Avenue
New York, NY 10016

Library of Congress Cataloging-in-Publication Data

Richardson, Joy.
Reptiles / by Joy Richardson.
p. cm. — (Picture science)
Includes index.
Summary: Text, photographs, and drawings explore the world of reptiles.
ISBN 0-531-14254-X
1. Reptiles — Juvenile literature. [1. Reptiles.] I. Title.
II. Series: Richardson, Joy. Picture science.
QL644.2.R53 1993
597.9—dc20 92-32912 CIP AC

10 9 8 7 6 5 4 3 2 1

Editor: Sarah Ridley
Designer: Janet Watson
Picture researcher: Sarah Moule
Illustrator: Angela Owen

Photographs: Bruce Coleman Ltd 7tl, 7tr, 13, 15, 21; Frank Lane Picture Agency front cover, title page, 16, 23, 27; Natural History Photographic Agency 7br, 18, 24; Oxford Scientific Films/Animals Animals 7bl, 8, 10.



Printed in Malaysia

PICTURE SCIENCE

# REPTILES

Joy Richardson

FRANKLIN WATTS
New York • Chicago • London • Toronto • Sydney

# Reptile relatives

Snakes and lizards,
crocodiles and alligators,
tortoises and turtles
are all reptiles.

There were reptiles on Earth
long before there were any people.

The biggest reptiles of all
were the dinosaurs.

Most reptiles today are quite small,
but all reptiles have bodies
that work in the same kind of way.

# Laying eggs

Reptile mothers lay eggs
and hide them out of sight.

The eggs are soft and leathery.

Baby reptiles break out of
their egg with the help of
an egg tooth on their snout.
This tooth drops off later.

The newborn babies look
like little adults.
They can run about and feed
themselves right from the start.
Most get no help from their parents.

# Growing bigger



Most reptiles shed their skin as they grow bigger. The colorless top layer of skin comes loose from the brightly colored skin below.

Snakes turn their old skin inside out as they wriggle free. They leave an empty tube behind.

Lizard skins crack and flake off.

# Tough skins

Reptiles have tough skin,
covered with horny scales
rather like fingernails.

This helps to keep them
from drying out in the heat.

Most reptiles cannot move very fast,
so tough, scaly skin helps
to protect them from enemies.

It would be a hard job biting through
a crocodile's armor-plated skin.

Slow-moving tortoises hide from
danger inside their thick, bony shell.

# Color and camouflage

Many reptiles are well camouflaged.
Their skin fits in with the
color of their surroundings.

Speckled lizards hide
easily on sandy rocks.

Patterned snakes slither unseen
among stones and leaves.

Many reptiles can change color.
Chameleons can change color very quickly
as they creep up on insects or
when they feel frightened.

# Temperature control

All reptiles are cold-blooded.
Their temperature depends on
the temperature outside.

Reptiles cannot keep themselves warm,
so they live mainly in hot places.

Reptiles are active only when
their temperature feels right.

In between they take long rests.
They lie in the sun to warm up
and hide in the shade to cool down.

In winter, reptiles hibernate
and do nothing until the
weather warms them up again.

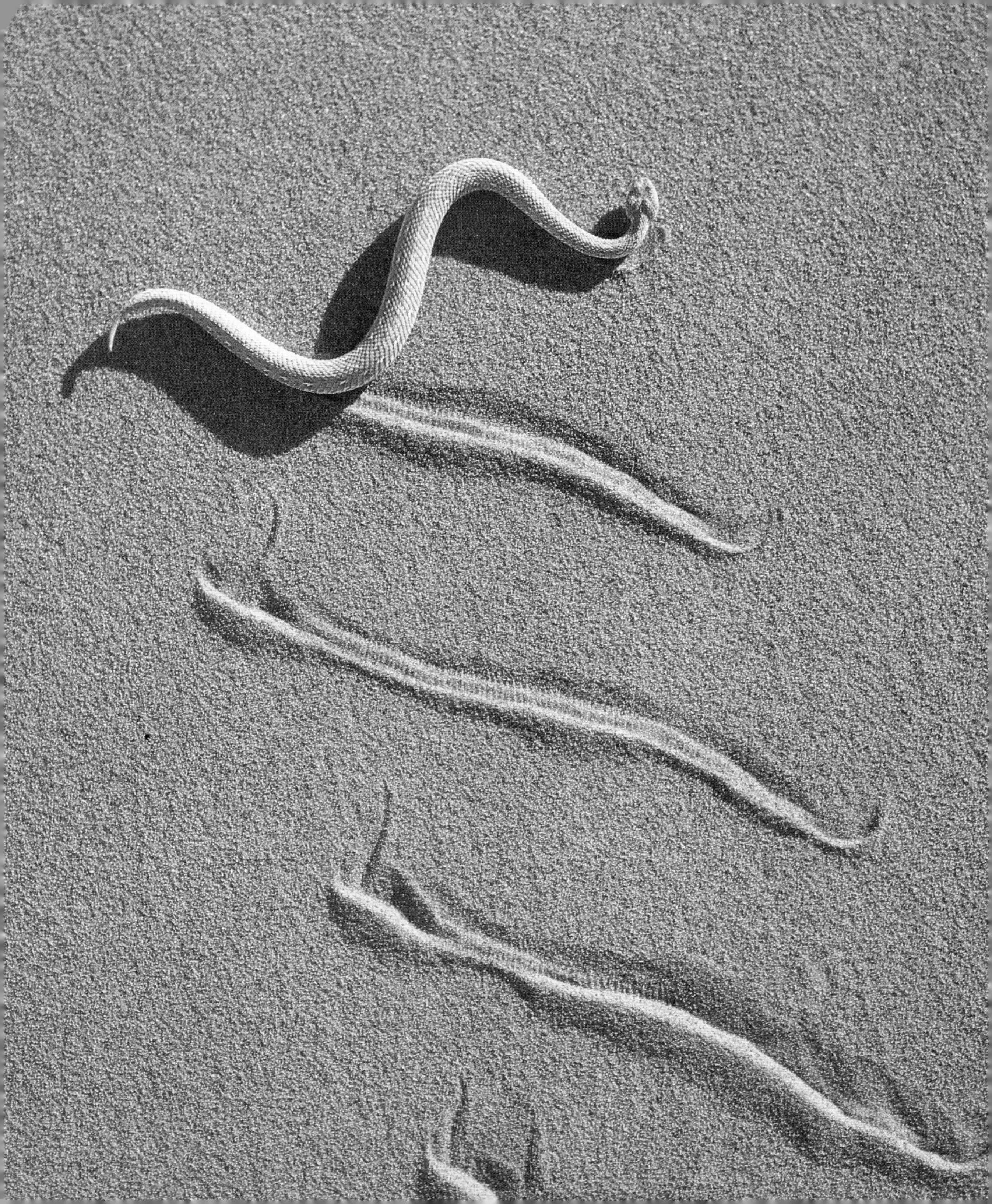

# Skeletons

All reptiles have a skeleton inside.
They have a backbone from head to tail
and most have four legs.

Snakes have no legs but
they have hundreds of tiny
bones in their backbone.
This makes them very flexible.
They can bend and wiggle and coil up.

Lizards scurry along with legs
sticking out on each side.
They can break off their tail and
leave it behind if they are attacked.

**Snake skeleton**

# On land and in water

Reptiles are land creatures
but some like the water.

Crocodiles and alligators
live in rivers and swamps and
use their tails for swimming.

They lay eggs on the land
and crawl around on their
stomach and stumpy legs.

Turtles come out of the sea
to lay their eggs in the sand.
The baby turtles flap their
way back to the sea
as quickly as possible.

# Eating a meal

Reptiles have jaws that
open really wide to catch food.

Snakes have a stretchy mouth.
They can swallow creatures whole.

Some snakes inject victims
with poison from their teeth.
Some snakes curl around
and squeeze them to death.

Snakes digest their food slowly.
They can go for weeks between meals.

Reptiles use no energy keeping warm,
so they do not need much to eat.

# Sight, sound, and smell

Most reptiles have eyes that
always stay open.

Snakes' eyes are covered
with transparent eyelids,
so they never need to blink.

Reptiles have sound openings on
their head but no ear flaps.

They have nostrils to
breathe air into their lungs.

Snakes and lizards flick out long
tongues to find smells in the air.

# Growing old

Most animals stop growing
when they become adults.

Reptiles never stop growing.

A tortoise's shell grows
bigger each year except
while it is hibernating.

This makes yearly growth rings
that help to show its age.

Some giant tortoises can
live to be over a hundred.

# Reptile ways

The tiniest lizard,
the longest snake,
the slowest tortoise,
and the fiercest crocodile
all have some things in common.

All reptiles lay eggs.
They have dry scaly skins.
They are cold-blooded.

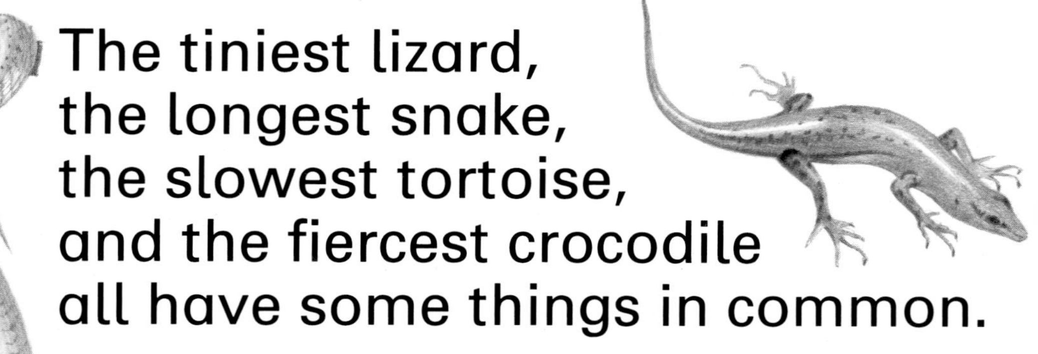

# Index

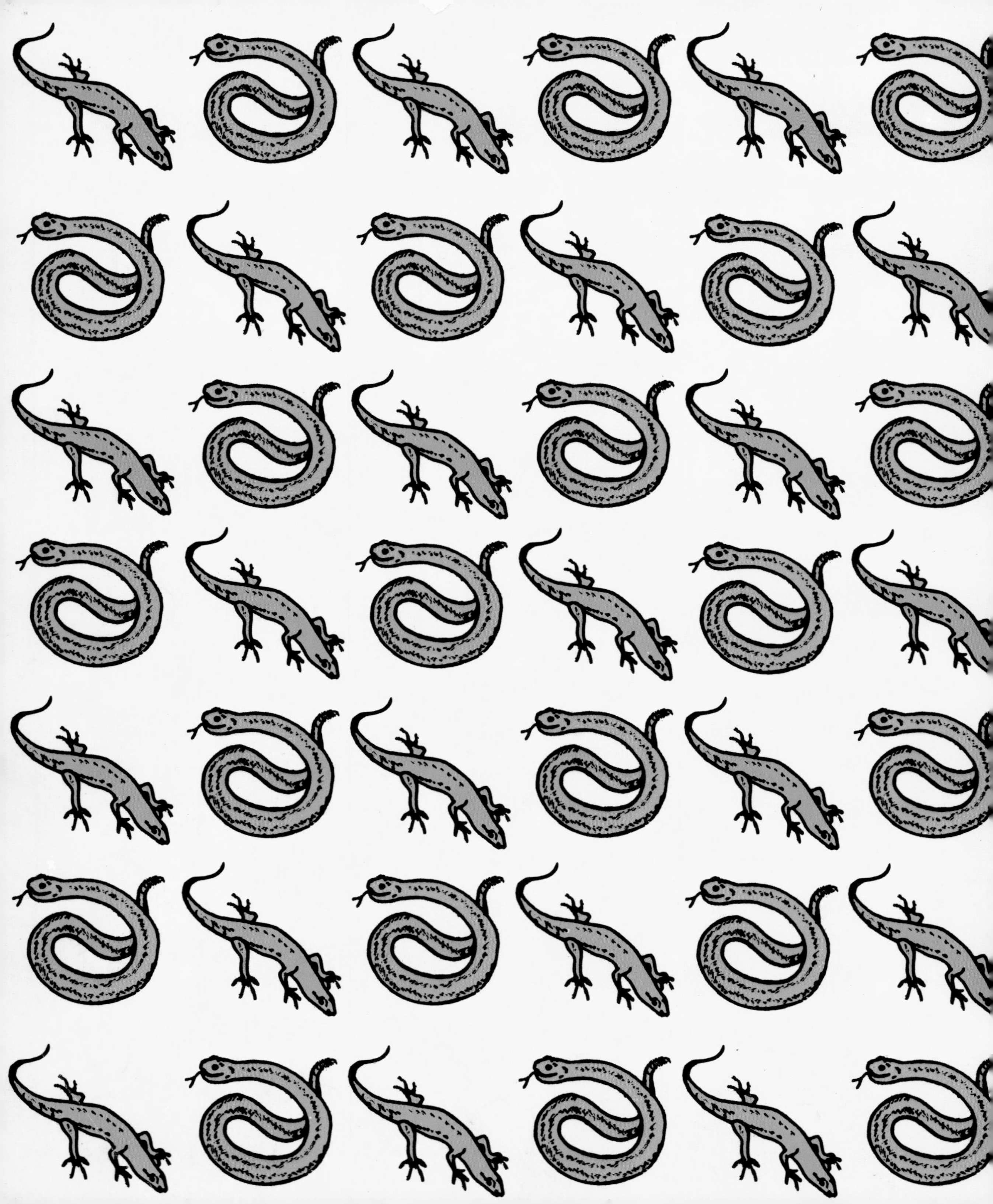

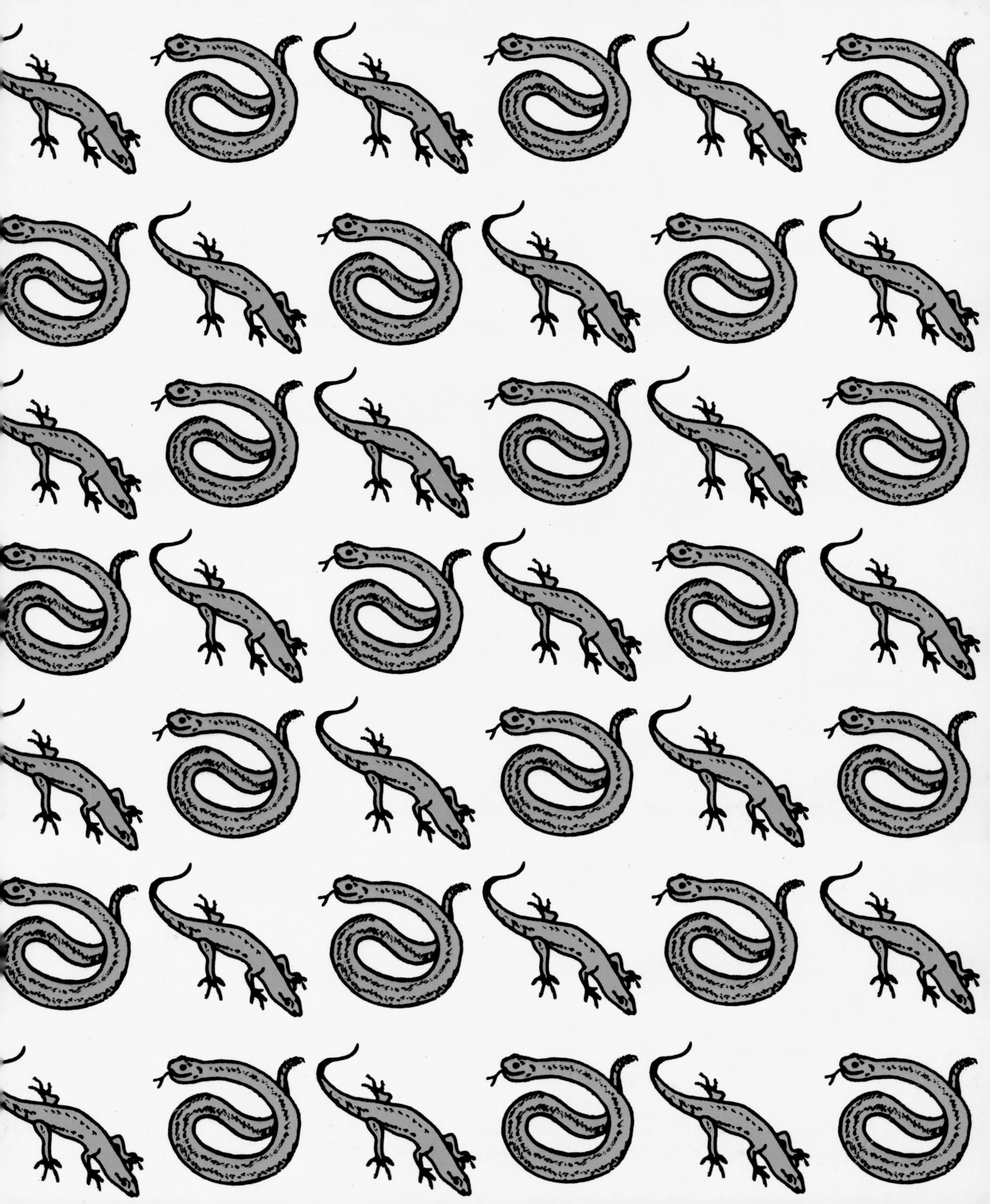